Elder Moon

A Memoir Told in Poems

by

Cyra Sweet Dumitru

Finishing Line Press
Georgetown, Kentucky

Elder Moon

A Memoir Told in Poems

Dedicated to Barbara Dumitru,
My dear friend & mother-in-law
October 27, 1927—July 12, 2014

Copyright © 2019 by Cyra Sweet Dumitru
ISBN 978-1-63534-856-9 First Edition
All rights reserved under International and Pan-American Copyright Conventions. No part of this book may be reproduced in any manner whatsoever without written permission from the publisher, except in the case of brief quotations embodied in critical articles and reviews.

ACKNOWLEDGMENTS

Some of these poems have appeared in:

Pecan Grove Review
Voices de la Luna
Poetry on The Move: San Antonio VIA Buses
Texas Poetry Calendar 2015

"Reason Not to Dust" first appeared in *Enchantment of the Ordinary Anthology*, Mutabilis Press

Gratitude to Martha Grant and Julia Jarrell whose open-hearted and attentive readings of an early draft of *Elder Moon* were instrumental in helping the collection find its beginning and unified point of view.

Publisher: Leah Maines
Editor: Christen Kincaid
Cover Art: Dan Dumitru
Author Photo: Analicia Lucia Perez
Cover Design: Leah Huete

Printed in the USA on acid-free paper.
Order online: www.finishinglinepress.com
also available on amazon.com

Author inquiries and mail orders:
Finishing Line Press
P. O. Box 1626
Georgetown, Kentucky 40324
U. S. A.

Table of Contents

FOREWORD
As Though 1
You as the Other Woman 2
Stroke Diary 3
Back Home Again in South Texas 8
Listening 9
Night Rose 10
Closing Down Your Home 11
Sleeping on the Floor of Mom's Unsold House 12
Elder Moon 13
Distance Between Illness and Home 14
Wakeful 15
Sound of Slipping Slowly Away 16
Speaking to Uncertainty 17
Near the Marianist Brothers' Cemetery on Campus 18
Upon Touching the Image of Jesus on the Stained Glass
    Window: I Pray for You 19
Measure of Acceptance 20
Eloquence 21
Sitting with Final Light 22
Release Following the Fall 23
Seen From Your Hospital Window 24
Hours After Your Passing 25
Afternoon of the Funeral: Amish Inn 26
What We Didn't Tell You 27
This New Sound 28
Reason Not to Dust 29
Keeping Bird Feeders Full 30

FOREWORD

Over the course of 30 years, my mother-in-law became my dear friend, and truly a second mother. She was born Barbara Stepetich to working-class immigrant parents, and lived all her life in Massillon, Ohio. I met her son and only child in Cincinnati, and we have lived most of our married life in San Antonio, Texas. Because Mom and I lived many miles apart in separate regions, it took time for us to get to know one another well.

It was during struggle that I discovered the loyal heart that was my mother-in-law. Mom was looking forward to becoming a grandmother, and I was her only chance for producing biological offspring. As years of infertility persisted, and as discouragement and loss mounted, I felt bereft. I also believed I was disappointing my in-laws. My own parents were already grandparents, thanks to my older brother and his wife. One day, Mom found me outside her ranch style home, crying. Another failed procedure. "I love you as my daughter," she said hugging me. "You and Danny are enough!" I breathed a little easier following her gracious words of acceptance.

Eventually, our children were born! When they were small, my husband traveled frequently. As there was no family in San Antonio to help while Dan was away, Mom often flew to San Antonio to help me manage the juggling act of tending home and having a professional life. Those years were her happiest, and she was a blessing to me.

As our children grew, Dan traveled less, and his parents aged. Mom's energy became absorbed by her husband who developed dementia, and eventually suffered a stroke. Mom cared for Dad at home without assistance, and at the cost of her own strength; she was in her early eighties when he died peacefully.

When Mom experienced her own stroke two years following Dad's death, she endured multiple complications as a consequence to the stroke, including persistent depression. Each health crisis diminished her physical strength and spiritual resilience.

For us, the distance between Ohio and Texas became such an obstacle. We were Mom's only family, and she did not want to leave the town of her birth. Besides, we could not duplicate in San Antonio the quality of personalized, compassionate, and affordable care provided by the assisted living facility in Massillon.

Dan and I made countless trips over the course of five years; some trips were planned and others unfolded as immediate response to health crises. It was easy to resent the situation: vacations foregone for years, driving rental cars in storms and blizzards, shoveling snow from the driveway with a broom, cost of hotel rooms once Mom's house was sold, grading papers on airplanes, desperately making up for cancelled classes upon return home.

Determined not to resent Mom and to keep my heart open, I journaled and wrote poems throughout each visit, each crisis. The writing process was medicinal. It helped me to pay attention lovingly and not feel numbed. Instead, I felt the privilege of witnessing intimately her vulnerability: flickers of humor within frustration and sadness, a slowly eroding will to fight, her surprisingly beautiful back as I bathed her while she sat on the edge of a hospital bed.

For me, this collection of poems embodies the healing truth voiced by my mentor and poetry therapist John Fox in his book *Poetic Medicine*, "Poetry is a natural medicine . . . Poetry helps us to feel our lives rather than be numb. The page, touched with our poem, becomes a place for painful feelings to be held, explored and transformed. Writing and reading poems is a way of seeing and naming where we have been, where we are and where we are going with our lives."

These poems are vital acts of witness that helped me to be patient and mindful with Mom regardless of the situation. These poems generated hope and creative energy by minimizing my sense of helplessness. They allowed me to accept ongoing sadness and release resentment, allowed me to offer devotion and celebrate small victories, allowed me to cherish my husband's attentive and endearing actions, and allowed me to receive

Mom's steadfast love on an entirely new level. I am profoundly grateful for the deep connection I shared with my mother-in-law, and for the relational beauty I experienced during her difficult, final years.

July 2018

AS THOUGH
With thanks to Kay Ryan

As though one stunned mockingbird
gradually regaining her wings
makes any difference to the sky,
as though clouds would miss
one less bird passing by.

                    As though
lifting one slat of a wooden blind
could console the trembling heart,
as though one streak of light through
a window might stir
                          a sunrise.

As though one burgeoning plant
could define a ceramic pot as garden,
name any green thing as hopeful.
As though gardens are always visible.

YOU AS THE OTHER WOMAN

A few months before Dad's death, he tells me
that when you disappear in the silver car,
this other woman shows up, and refuses to serve
him supper. She hides his envelope of dollars.
When he pounds the wall, she rushes into
his son's room, shuts the door and cries.

* *

The following day, Dad's refugee mind quiets:
Soviet tanks pushing through Constanza fall
from sight; machine guns are stilled.
The police who once inquired after him vanish.

The bird bright on the branch is a *cardinal*.
The old woman raking leaves is you,
his loyal wife.

For a full, lovely morning
he savors the autumn air.

STROKE DIARY
    for my mother-in-law

When we first see you
in MICU, you are wordless
in a neighboring country—a wide
muddy river dividing us.

One side of your face unmoved
and mask-like, the other side
is upturned as if caught
by surprise.

    Day 2
The next day you choke on jello
while the nurse feeds you.

    Day 3
You lift your right hand,
your right leg, and walk
with assistance.

Your son writes simple questions
on unlined paper, draws boxes
around "Yes" "No".

"Are you in pain?"
You point: No

"Do you know who I am?"   Yes

"Do you feel hopeful?"
Hand lifts, considers, drops.

Day 4
You press your tongue against palate
and speak, "no".
You swallow vanilla pudding
and bits of scrambled egg

Day 5
"Th e r a p i s t"
the muddy river thins
to a stream.

Day 6
The first sentence feels like wildflowers
blooming in sand after steady rain.

When you can't summon the right word,
you shake your head as if erasing.

Try again.
                Shake your head.
                              Fall silent.

Day 7
The speech therapist gives you worksheets:

Park the car in the	garbage garage umbrella.
It is time to shovel the	bathtub driveway blanket.
Hang the dress in the	closet snow window.

We open the closet in your hospital room,
hold up blouses on hangers. Explain.

You persist, read slowly, select the logical word,
pause, then say, "I am confused."

Day 8
We watch you waken and startle,
survey the room for clues:

crisp edges, clean lines that distinguish
where walls end and solid floor begins.

Where to take hold

Day 9
Cut flowers fall onto
hospital floor. Glass
vase caught at last
moment, water cascades.

As I gather scattered snapdragons
and solitary rose, you murmur
bruised from your bed,
"just throw the flowers away."

Days 10 & 11
Day of therapy, dinner. Tired:
"I wish I would just die.
I wish I would just die."

We chime in, change the inflection,
tap out a rhythm on the table.
"I wish   I would   just die.
I wish   I would   just die."

Day 21
"It is a beautiful day.
Sun shines," you say.

"My blinds are closed.
My blinds are closed because
I can't taste anything I eat.
Not even strawberry jam on my toast."

"So closing the blinds
will cure your taste buds?" we ask.

"Yes."

Day 22
I fill your room with bubbles
that bloom from a tiny wand,
as I blow gently.

Delicate zeroes filled with my breath,
press against the window, search
the horizon before popping.

You refuse to open your eyes.

Where are any of us now?
Mistaking the full moon
for zero?

Day 23
A cardinal sings green
from the low branch of a willow tree;
you sit outside with eyes closed.

In the singing air you forget
that you can no longer taste
the scrambled eggs and

red velvet cake; forget
that your head shakes along
with your hand lifting the fork;

forget that the night is
a mouth unhinged and
swallowing you.

Day 25
"I want to be healthy again.
Since my stroke, my mind is dead
and now my body is so stupid!"

BACK HOME AGAIN IN SOUTH TEXAS

Everywhere the drought:
strips of bare ground cracking.

Resonant the one recent rain:
green still alive in collapsed grass.

Wondrous your new small word as
your mind slowly recalls.

LISTENING

In the stillness of night
as the moon shines a thin claw,
I am wakened by a shadow-sound
at the edge of hearing—

great horned owl names its place among these hills.

When the owl falls silent,
my own breath lifts
and lowers—listening
for the space that names me.

NIGHT ROSE

A full moon blooms
upon my kitchen table
petal by creamy petal.

CLOSING DOWN YOUR HOME

Not much remains
in your well-kept home.
The orange chairs that cheered
the living room now brighten
your room at the Village.
Other furniture shipped
or given away.

We drain water from the pipes:
winter approaches. Turn
the heat down low, lock up.

Snow will pile soon in the yard,
the driveway. Leave it to the sun.

SLEEPING ON THE FLOOR OF MOM'S UNSOLD HOUSE

Today you believed you would die alone.

In your deafness you heard
a doctor say *blood count zero*.
So you watched the clock and prayed.

When I finally arrive,
plane delayed by storms,
you cling to me and weep.

*

Just before midnight, I enter your dark house:
ready for your son's orange sleeping bag.
Little receives me other than
the chair at the kitchen counter
and artificial candles—
timed lights placed two years ago
when you were newly widowed.

They flicker along windowsills
and on the mantle above the fireplace,
silent words that comfort.
I follow their small light
inward through darkness,
find a candle burning
on the lone dresser
in the bedroom.

The furnace bangs and breathes
from the basement, wafting warmth
upward.
   Timed lights,
whatever you are made of,
guard our surrenders to the dark.

ELDER MOON

The beauty of your octogenarian skin
curving creamy as a summer moon
along your shoulders and back

bare before the warm washcloth
I hold as I bathe you—sitting
on the edge of a hospital bed:

the delicate spaces we stumble upon
when frailty comes calling.

DISTANCE BETWEEN ILLNESS AND HOME

Your days turn white
and confined as you return
to the hospital.

Your voice shortens, pulls into
the lonely nest of your heart,
shocked today, back into sinus rhythm.

This morning we held your hand
until the doctor arrived, urged you
to fight.   Now,
we watch fire trucks blast toward
the courthouse of Terre Haute,
as we make our slow driving way
from northern Ohio to south Texas.

Each day we travel new terrain,
mile by mile. A hawk glides
across a snowy field.

This world is never one place:
high ground, uneven field,
valleys of shadow.

WAKEFUL

The dark hours unbend long and ragged.
I am wakeful alongside them,

thinking of you: a wanderer
who has lost her centering stone.

I dream of searching,
unearthing the hidden stone:

a body that you can work again.

SOUND OF SLIPPING SLOWLY AWAY

Each day you slip a little
                      further from yourself:
shadow of the oak tree losing
                      one more bend of a branch.

SPEAKING TO UNCERTAINTY

It seems you are everywhere:
stationed calmly in a corner
or in tree shadow, working

your sketchpad and charcoals,
pastels that never dwindle,
tracing outlines of possibilities,

giving rise to nuanced light
and delicate shadings, working
with elegant confidence

while I wrestle with concerns.
Do you hesitate to render
what your mind's eye sees?

Your hand feels steady
upon the canvas of my life—
my open, unknowing

and hungry life.

NEAR THE MARIANIST BROTHERS' CEMETERY ON CAMPUS

Long pipes of the towering wind
chimes resound from the pecan tree:
devotion, devotion.
I close my eyes.
Let   vibration   open:

at last I can   cry our sorrow

the burden of love
when life is stubborn habit,
neurons firing—breath
blind to joy:

wind   chimes   stir

UPON TOUCHING THE IMAGE OF JESUS ON THE STAINED GLASS WINDOW: I PRAY FOR YOU

Inside Assumption Chapel:
another day of wind and
the underside of winter stones.

Such blaze: almost unbearable
as I brush my hand across
folds of his flowing cloak.

Flame leaps from colored glass to fingers:
I stand burning and timeless
from some invisible root.

"Is it you who touched my robe?"
He locks his eyes onto mine
with such oceanic kindness

I can neither speak nor look away.
He lifts my hand still warm
from his garment,

adds yet another heat
by placing my hand between his,
like a loaf of bread baking.

His radiant breath fills the air like a wave:
"Your faith has healed you, woman.
Go in peace."

MEASURE OF ACCEPTANCE

stirs, like a creekbed
that collects and holds
slow risings.

You look up

from stillness, ask me
to lift the blinds, notice
wild daisies glowing.

ELOQUENCE

As your heart muscle weakens
and your body edges
toward stone,
the lit wick of your spirit
brightens and lifts.

"When I didn't know better," you laugh,
remembering some former fretfulness.

As your son reaches
to switch on the nebulizer,
he stops:
leans toward you,
rests his forehead upon yours.
Mother/son hold and fill.

Nothing is spoken.
Everything is said.

SITTING WITH FINAL LIGHT

Sitting with light at end
of the day, as last
radiance softens

hollows of the large stones,
glistens the underside
of wax myrtle leaves.

The salvia sing about morning
rain. Mockingbird throats a dazzle
of rhythms, pauses, bathes the air again.

Woodpecker lands on the small oak
where a grandson's red swing
once hung from a bough—

its tapping steady as heartbeat.

RELEASE FOLLOWING THE FALL

By the time we arrive at your side,
you have drifted away from words,
demands upon breath.

Where can we touch you?
Where will your fractured limbs
not recoil from pain?

I rest my forehead upon yours—
that damp field above your oxygen mask,
close my eyes.

Recalling words from the haiku master,
I unshore the lake of my heart, ask
my waters to mingle with yours,

gather ache of broken bones,
traces of fear and regret
so I can sweep such debris

through me, breathe it out, out.
Breathe in the lake of our love,
your resolve that now finally is

season of release. All I hear
for certain while our foreheads touch
is water unfurling the cup of itself.

SEEN FROM YOUR HOSPITAL WINDOW

turning away momentarily
from broken-white sheets
constant sound of oxygen
silent etchings of heart monitor

nothing to be done:

white sea horse drifts
in a blue ocean-sky

HOURS AFTER YOUR PASSING

Slowly the orange and electric pinks
fade at sunset's horizon;
my hand still holds your heat.

AFTERNOON OF THE FUNERAL: THE AMISH INN

Minutes after the Amish woman
collects apples fallen to the ground,
walks away with brimming buckets—
two more apples drop
from the laden branches.

WHAT WE DIDN'T TELL YOU

I would have understood
you say to me in a dream.

I wish I could tell you
we never doubted
that you would still love
your grandson, accept him
despite the teachings
of your church.

Rather, we sought to protect you:
heart already heavy with cares,
tremor worsening, shy about
lifting a fork in front of others
because of spillage.

You would have had good reason
to not trust the world
with your grandson's light:

threatening note left at his seat
on the middle school bus
following the driver's public taunt.

Other things I will not tell you
even now. Now I need you
to help protect him.

THIS NEW SOUND

Window open on a mild April day,
shimmering clouds.   Deep sky.

A long rough road closes behind us.
A soft wind carries tidings of kindness.

Ice cubes shift in my glass, sound
like syllables melting: *Amen*

REASON NOT TO DUST

Let there be shiver of recognition
as we slide our fingers along
windowsills and bookshelves,
tops of kitchen cabinets.

Let fingertips feel kinship with
what has settled: drifted
unseen through open doors.
Let us see ourselves

in this delicate shedding,
memory of skin,
infinite debris of stars:
what we will become—

slightly heavier than breath,
levitating lightly upon wind

KEEPING BIRD FEEDERS FULL

> *"Hope is the thing with feathers-*
> *that perches in the soul-*
> *and sings the tune without the words-*
> *and never stops—at all—"* Emily Dickinson

Again and again Emily Dickinson lands
on feathered wings in our backyard—
red bloom of cardinals and blue
streak of scrub jays, flicker of yellow
as the oriole keeps to a distant juniper.

Such bright-singing-wings
flow in and out of sight, unaware
of watchfulness from the window.
The cardinal does not know, as he rides
the wooden feeder rocking in southern wind,

that the seed he eats sings of human presence.
These feeders hanging from the Ponderosa
pine and triangle of crepe myrtles bespeak
love, invitation to linger, hunger
for cadences to thread the gray air.

When your son fills them every few days,
he fills me too. How does he know
how much my heart needs
this serenade of color,
this sustenance of song?

North wind presses upon the pine
needles, rocks mockingbird
with his gifted ear. Day
brightens. Shadows loosen
from the bark, scattering
bits of seed.

Cyra Sweet Dumitru has written poetry all her life. For 18 years, she has taught poetry writing, composition, and writing as wellness courses at St. Mary's University in San Antonio, Texas. She is also a Certified Poetic Medicine Practitioner, through The Institute for Poetic Medicine founded by John Fox. In this capacity, she offers therapeutic poetry circles to: college students struggling with mental health issues, women veterans, LGBTQ teenagers, and to adults seeking to articulate their experience of being an embodied soul. She is the author of three full-length collections of poems: *What the Body Knows* (Pecan Grove Press), *Listening to Light* (River Lily Press) and *Remains* (Pecan Grove Press).

www.ingramcontent.com/pod-product-compliance
Lightning Source LLC
LaVergne TN
LVHW041600070426
835507LV00011B/1215